GOD'S OWN PEOPLE
Studies in 1 Peter

TOGETHER IN FAITH SERIES
Learner Session Guide

Tom Teichmann

Minneapolis

GOD'S OWN PEOPLE: STUDIES IN 1 PETER
Learner Session Guide

Together in Faith Series
Book of Faith Adult Bible Studies

Copyright © 2011 Augsburg Fortress. All rights reserved. Except for brief quotations in critical articles or reviews, no part of this book may be reproduced in any manner without prior written permission from the publisher. For more information, visit: www.augsburgfortress.org/copyrights or write to: Permissions, Augsburg Fortress, Box 1209, Minneapolis, MN 55440-1209.

 Book of Faith is an initiative of the
Evangelical Lutheran Church in America
God's work. Our hands.

For more information about the Book of Faith initiative, go to www.bookoffaith.org.

Scripture quotations, unless otherwise marked, are from New Revised Standard Version Bible, copyright © 1989 Division of Christian Education of the National Council of Churches of Christ in the United States of America. Used by permission. All rights reserved.

Web site addresses are provided in this resource for your use. These listings do not represent an endorsement of the sites by Augsburg Fortress, nor do we vouch for their content for the life of this resource.

ISBN: 978-1-4514-0124-0
Writer: Tom Teichmann
Cover and interior design: Spunk Design Machine, spkdm.com
Typesetting: Running Design Group, Minneapolis, MN

The paper used in this publication meets the minimum requirements of American National Standard for Information Sciences—Permanence of Paper for Printed Library Materials, ANSI Z329.48-1984.

Manufactured in the U.S.A.
14 13 12 11 1 2 3 4 5 6 7 8 9 10

CONTENTS

1   A Tested People   5
1 Peter 1:3–9

2   A Trusting People   11
1 Peter 1:17–23

3   A Called People   17
1 Peter 2:19–25

4   A Holy People   23
1 Peter 2:2–10

5   A Proclaiming People   29
1 Peter 3:13–22

SESSION ONE

1 Peter 1:3–9

Learner Session Guide

Focus Statement
As we strive to lead godly lives, there are times when our actions provoke a negative reaction from others. In those times the living hope given through Christ's resurrection can sustain us.

Key Verse
Blessed be the God and Father of our Lord Jesus Christ! By his great mercy he has given us a new birth into a living hope through the resurrection of Jesus Christ from the dead. 1 Peter 1:3

A Tested People

Focus Image

God has given us a living hope through Christ's resurrection. © iStockphoto

Gather

Check-in

Welcome! Take this time to connect or reconnect with the others in your group.

Pray

(L=Leader; R=Response)

L: *God, we come together to explore the book of faith, your word.*
R: *Open our minds, Lord!*
L: *Let the history behind the scriptures lead us to further knowledge.*
R: *Open our hearts, Lord!*
L: *Let these ancient words speak to us today in meaningful, exciting ways.*
R: *Open our mouths, Lord!*
L: *Let our discussion be lively, respectful, and engaging.*
R: *Open our lives, Lord!*
L: *Let us carry the gift of a living hope into our communities. Amen.*

SESSION ONE

 Notes

Focus Activity

For each question below, raise your right hand to answer "yes," and your left to answer "no." Be ready to give a reason for your opinion.

- As followers of Jesus, are we ever called to act in ways that are countercultural?
- Is the world opposed to all the ideals of Christianity?
- Do we sometimes experience a backlash for acting as Jesus would have us act?
- If we experience a negative reaction for following Jesus, does this constitute "suffering"?

Open Scripture

Read 1 Peter 1:3–9.

- What words and/or phrases stand out for you on the initial reading of this text?

- What do you think the writer means by "suffer various trials" and "tested by fire"?

- What in this portion of the letter encourages you?

Join the Conversation

Literary Context

1. The Bible contains many genres or types of literature. This book, 1 Peter, falls under the genre of epistle or letter. In many ways it is like any letter you might write to a family member or friend. In some distinctive ways it is not.

- Read 1 Peter 1:3–9. Make a list of the similarities and differences between this text and a letter or e-mail message you might send someone.

SESSION ONE

2. An epistle has three parts: the opening, main body, and closing. The opening contains the *prescript* and thanksgiving. The prescript lists the sender's name and titles, names the addressee(s), and offers a salutation. The main body of an epistle begins with a short summary of what is to come, and continues with a logical argument designed to meet the writer's goals. The closing summarizes the main point again, offers greetings, and gives final instructions and benedictions.

- Review 1 Peter 1:3–9 again, and skim the sections immediately before and after it. What parts of an epistle do you see?

Historical Context

1. Peter, one of Jesus' twelve disciples, went on to become a leader in the early church. It is difficult to determine, however, whether he is the writer of 1 Peter. In ancient times writing under someone else's name was an acceptable practice, especially for a student writing in the name of a great teacher. Scholars offer evidence for and against Peter writing this epistle, including the use of language, the historical context, the content, the time of the writing, and the literary style.

- How does the idea that Peter himself may not have actually written this epistle affect your attitude towards it? How might the Word of God be present in words written by someone other than Peter?

2. Knowing some of the history lying behind a Bible text can help us more fully understand what the text is saying. This often involves finding out what we can about the first hearers or readers of the text—about their culture, economy, religion, and so on (sometimes called their *Sitz im Leben*, a German phrase for "setting in life").

- Read 1 Peter 1:1–9. What can you determine about the people to whom this epistle is written?

Notes

SESSION ONE

Notes

Lutheran Context

1. Lutherans look at the Bible through the lenses of both law and gospel. The law is about what God asks of us, while the gospel is about what God does for us.

- Review 1 Peter 1:3-9 and decide which words or phrases sound like law to you, and which sound like gospel to you. Use the chart below to list your choices.

Law	Gospel

2. 1 Peter is written to people who have been given "a new birth" and "a living hope" (1:3) in Christ. They were perishable, now they are imperishable. They were defiled, now they are undefiled. This new identity is a *paradox*—it holds two seemingly opposite things to be true at the same time. In talking about this paradox, Martin Luther said we are simultaneously saints and sinners, claimed and saved by God, yet continuing to sin.

- How do you understand this new identity given to you? In what ways do you reveal your new identity to the world?

Devotional Context

1. Look at the Focus Image at the beginning of this session. Consider what this picture says to you about new birth, living hope, baptism, or hope in the midst of suffering.

- Where is God in this picture, and what is God calling you or your congregation to do? Write down your thoughts about this, using capital letters for words that give you hope, and small letters for words that describe suffering as you have experienced it.

SESSION ONE

 Notes

- Look again at 1 Peter 1:3–9. Place an asterisk next to words or phrases which you would describe as the "snow." Underline words or phrases which you would describe as the "flowers."

2. List some songs or hymns that convey the same message of living hope that is presented in 1 Peter 1:3–9. Pick one or two of these songs to sing together if you wish.

Wrap-up

Be ready to look back over the work your group has done in this session.

Pray

God of hope, make us new each day. New to proclaim your salvation throughout our community. New and sustained by living hope through Christ's ultimate victory over death and sin. New to rejoice in your promises in times of suffering or testing. We pray this through Jesus Christ our risen Savior and our living hope. Amen.

Go with God. Live and share what you have learned. Return hungry for more!

Extending the Conversation

Homework

1. Read the next session's Bible text: 1 Peter 1:17–23.

2. Take time during the next few weeks to read all five chapters of 1 Peter. (Don't worry! It won't take long—it's quite short.) Try reading sections of the epistle from more than one Bible translation (for example, Today's English Version, New International Version for Readers, or the Message). As you read, underline or highlight what you believe to be key passages and important words.

Enrichment

1. Epistles, though written, were intended to be spoken and heard. The writer generally dictated the words to a scribe. The finished epistle was not intended for a single recipient, but for the church. It was spoken to the church by someone who had memorized the content. The congregation heard the epistle then, similar to the way the scribe heard the writer.

SESSION ONE

2. If possible, memorize the Key Verse (p. 5) and say it to your pastor next Sunday. If that's too daunting, listen to the epistle as it's read in worship next week, instead of following along in a written text. And if that's not possible, have a family member read 1 Peter 1:3–9 to you several times as you listen carefully.

3. Skim through Luke and Acts, or look up the word *Peter* in a Bible concordance, to learn more about the disciple Peter's story—his previous job, family situation, experiences with Jesus, work as an evangelist after Pentecost, and so on. (Check your church library for a Bible concordance, or locate one that can be searched and studied online.)

4. Reflect on what Peter might say to encourage a pair of feuding friends or family members to forgive one another. You may want to write this down as a journaling exercise. Or write Peter's "curriculum vitae"—a list of all the important events in his life. For Peter, this list would start with "fisherman" and end with "crucified upside down."

For Further Reading

Apprenticed to Hope: A Sourcebook for Difficult Times by Julie E. Neraas (Augsburg Fortress, 2009).

Reason for Hope by José Luis Martín Descalzo (Augsburg Fortress, 2007).

SESSION TWO

1 Peter 1:17–23

Learner Session Guide

 **Focus Statement**

A multitude of worldly things and people vie for our allegiance, promising safety, health, fame, and fortune if we put our faith in them, but what they offer is transient. What God gives—Jesus—lasts forever and is worthy of trust.

Key Verse

Through [Jesus] you have come to trust in God, who raised him from the dead and gave him glory, so that your faith and hope are set on God.
1 Peter 1:21

A Trusting People

 **Focus Image**

Who can you trust? © Exactostock/SuperStock

Gather

Check-in

Take this time to connect or reconnect with the others in your group. Be ready to share new thoughts or insights about your last session.

Pray

God of re-birth and new life, your Son, Jesus, trusted you and was obedient unto death on a cross, and you glorified him by raising him up. Give us the faith and hope we need to trust in you above all things, as Jesus did. And by our obedience to your truth, make us holy as you are holy. Be with us as we study your word, that we might come to know you more deeply. Amen.

Focus Activity

Reflect on the Focus Image. Who or what do you trust? Finish the following sentences.

- I'd trust you with my personal belongings:
- I'd trust you with my money:

Session 2: 1 Peter 1:17–23   11

SESSION TWO

 Notes

- I'd trust you with my family:
- I'd trust you with my health:
- I'd trust you with my future:
- I'd trust you with my spiritual sensibilities:

Open Scripture

Read 1 Peter 1:17–23.

- As you listen, prepare to ask a question about a word or phrase or concept you found difficult.

- What reasons do those addressed have for putting their trust in God?

- If you were the one receiving this epistle, what stands out to you as being most important in this section?

Join the Conversation

Historical Context

1. Though Peter's epistle is thought to have been for distribution to all the early churches, it is addressed to the churches in Pontus, Galatia, Cappadocia, Asia, and Bithynia, all found in what we generally refer to as Asia Minor, part of Turkey. The writer says these fledgling churches are in "exile."

- Find the churches addressed in 1 Peter on the map on the next page. What do you notice about their locations? Why do you suppose churches were planted in this area? Why might they have been persecuted?

SESSION TWO

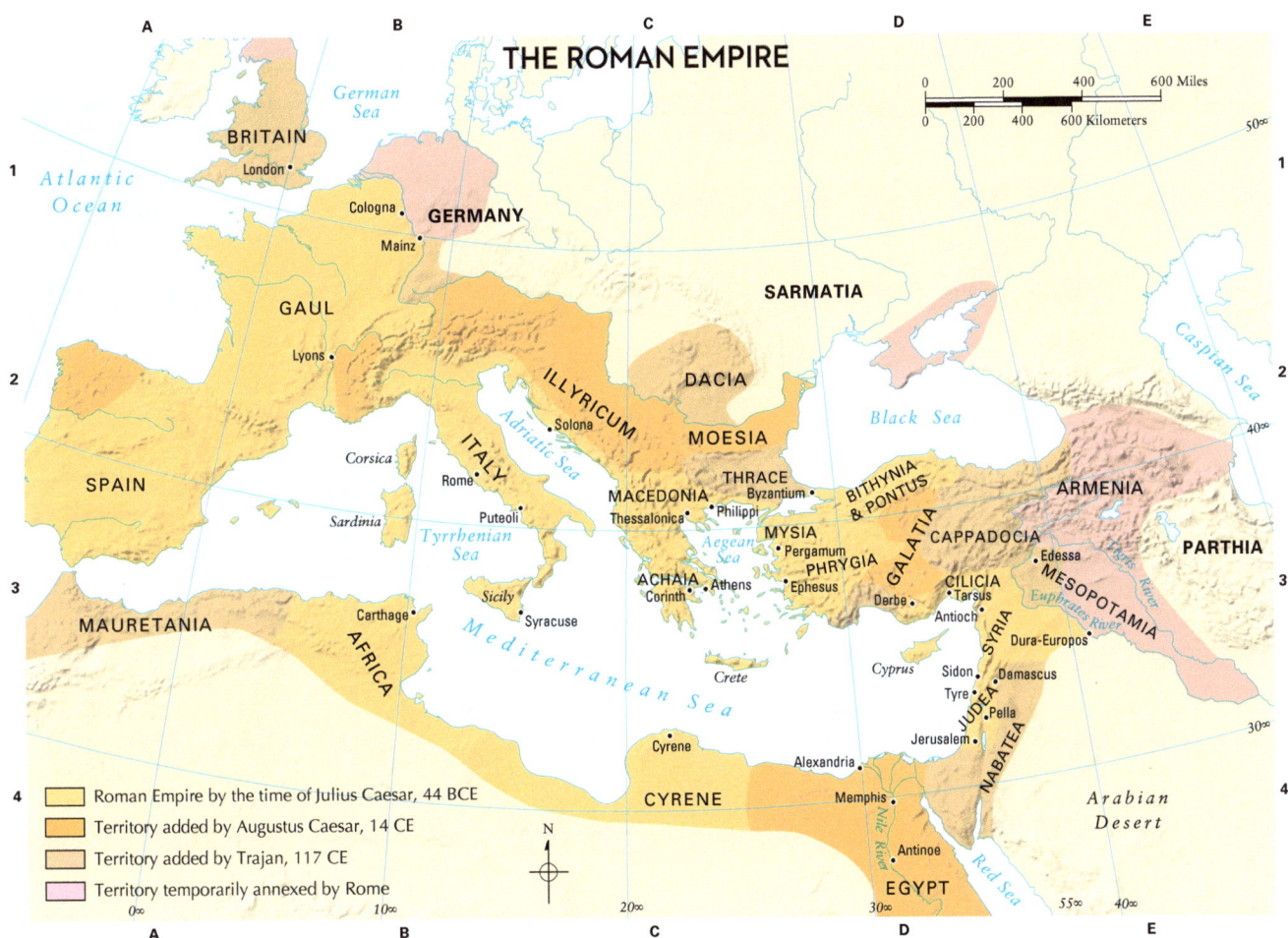

2. Some biblical scholars discern the presence of a baptismal liturgy behind the structure of an epistle. Today's text contains words and phrases that suggest this was part of the letter's *Sitz im Leben* or "setting in life."

- Read through the passage again, underlining words or phrases that remind you of baptism, and circling those which call to mind other liturgical dialogs or ritual actions. If you were an early Christian suffering persecution, how might the use of baptismal imagery in this letter affect you?

SESSION TWO

Notes

Literary Context

1. Epistles were written for a purpose, not just to say "hi" (although many do include personal greetings). The purpose was generally pastoral—the writer was concerned about a situation in the church and wished to address it. He would do so using up to three types of arguments structured by the rules of Greco-Roman rhetoric. 1 Peter uses each one: approving or condemning action (see 3:15–16), encouraging what is good and discouraging what is bad (see 1:3–13), and persuading people to follow a certain course of action (see 2:11–13).

- In 1 Peter 1:17–23, what most inspires you to understanding or action?

2. The writer sets up a dialog that compares the world and worldly ways with God's kingdom and God's ways.

- According to the text, what is greater or longer-lasting in each of the following pairs? Give explanations for your answers.

    | futility | completion |
    | silver or gold | Christ's blood |
    | hidden | revealed |
    | perishable | imperishable |

Lutheran Context

1. In 1 Peter 1:17, the writer advises the churches that if they invoke as Father the one who judges all impartially by their deeds, then they had better live in "reverent fear." This sounds like Luther's explanations of the Ten Commandments in his *Small Catechism*. Each explanation begins with, "We should fear and love God…." In the epistle and the catechism, the meaning of fear is about respect or holding something in awe.

- Why should the people live in reverent fear? What are the futile ways mentioned in 1:18? What makes trusting in God possible?

2. As Lutherans, we hold scripture up to scripture to better understand its meaning. Let's hold 1 Peter 1:17–23 up against a passage from one of Luther's favorite epistles—Romans 12:9–21.

- As the Romans text is read out loud sentence by sentence, raise your right hand when you hear something close to the same advice as the 1 Peter text. Raise your left hand if you hear something in Romans that contradicts 1 Peter. How does hearing Romans 12:9–21 help you better understand the 1 Peter text?

SESSION TWO

Devotional Context

1. Look over 1 Peter 1:17–23 again. What situation(s) does the writer address? What advantages do the people have, according to the text? What reasons are they given for trusting in God?

- If you wrote an epistle to your own church, what issues would you address, what advantages would you point out, and what reasons would you give for trusting in God?

2. Scripture is transformational—it changes you. Our response to hearing the gospel proclaimed in scripture is not passive. It involves action words—go, tell, share, serve, etc.

- Make a list of the top five or ten action words implied by 1 Peter 1:17–23. (The subject can be God, us, or the church.)

Wrap-up

Be ready to look back over the work your group has done in this session.

Pray

God, you are worthy of trust, more than the things we own, more than the rulers who rise and then fall away, more than retirement accounts, market portfolios, and IRAs, more than even ourselves. Help us to trust in you, not only in times of trial, but in times of joy, so that we might enjoy life abundantly. For you are our God, and we are your people. Amen.

Go with God. Trust in God's grace. Thanks be to God!

Extending the Conversation

Homework

1. Read the next session's Bible text: 1 Peter 2:19–25.

2. Look up the word *trust* in a Bible concordance. (A Bible concordance is a list of words and where they are used in the Bible. Some Bibles have an abridged concordance in the back.) Pick several of the verses that contain the word *trust*. Read them and write down any additional insights about trusting God.

3. Look at the lyrics to two traditional hymns, "Trust and Obey" (http://www.hymnal.net/hymn.php/h/582) and "If You But Trust in God to Guide You" (ELW 769, or http://sdahymnal.tripod.com/HTM/S510.html). How are the concepts of trusting and obeying similar in these hymns, and how are they different? Chart your responses. Which hymn is most like 1 Peter 1:17–23?

 Notes

SESSION TWO

Notes

4. Take key words from the session text and illustrate them according to their intended meaning in 1 Peter. Use whatever art medium you like—pencil, charcoal, collage, etc. Another option would be to "illuminate" the text of your favorite part of today's passage. (For definitions and examples of illuminated texts see http://en.wikipedia.org/wiki/Illuminated_manuscript.)

Enrichment

1. The session text says that Jesus was destined to be our savior "before the foundation of the world." How do you see destiny working in your life? God is the source of our destiny—does that mean that our path in life is basically a straight line we cannot veer away from if we are to end up in heaven? Can destiny be a bad thing? How do you understand God's role in that?

2. Gather a group together to view *Leap of Faith* (Paramount, 1992) for a "sideways look" at what it means to trust God. In this movie, Steve Martin plays a fraudulent faith healer who trusts only in the dollar and people's gullibility. He is shocked into re-examining his faithlessness when he is actually able to heal someone.

3. What does it mean to you that scripture is the "living and enduring word of God" (1 Peter 1:23)? What songs or hymns also talk about scripture in this way? (Browse through a hymnal or do an online search on "hymns songs God's word.")

For Further Reading

Speaking of Trust: Conversing with Luther about the Sermon on the Mount by Martin Marty (Augsburg Fortress, 2003).

Fortress Introduction to the New Testament by Gerd Theissen (Fortress Press, 2003). See chapter 1 for the literary form of epistles, and chapter 7 for the practice of writing under another person's name.

SESSION THREE

1 Peter 2:19–25

Learner Session Guide

Focus Statement
The life of a follower of Jesus is cruciform—patterned on the cross and its selfless implications. This is so different from the world's norm that as followers we are sometimes subject to suffering, but we don't bear the cross alone.

Key Verse
For to this you have been called, because Christ also suffered for you, leaving you an example, so that you should follow in his steps.
1 Peter 2:21

A Called People

 Focus Image

"Cross Wall" at Messiah Lutheran Church, Amherst, New Hampshire. © Tom Teichmann

Gather

Check-in
Welcome! Take this time to connect or reconnect with the others in your group. Be ready to share new thoughts or insights about your last session.

Pray
One: *Faithful God,*
Many: *Come among us, we pray.*
One: *You have given us faith, and tested that faith to make it pure.*
Many: *In you we can trust above all others.*
One: *We have been called to bear witness to the cross of Christ.*
Many: *Come among us, we pray. Come among us, make our hearts burn with the knowledge of your book of faith, that we might love one another with the selfless love of Christ. Amen.*

Focus Activity
Take a look at the Focus Image, a collection of crosses representing many styles, colors, materials, and interpretations. Think about other crosses you have seen. What type of cross is most meaningful to you, and why?

Session 3: 1 Peter 2:19–25   17

SESSION THREE

Notes

Open Scripture
Read 1 Peter 2:19–25.

- What comes to mind when you think about Jesus' call?

- What word or phrase in this text touches your heart?

- What questions do you have?

Join the Conversation
Historical Context

1. To read and understand 1 Peter 2:19–25, it's important to know that slavery was a common practice in ancient Mediterranean society. Under Rome, slavery began with household slaves and field workers, and grew as thousands of citizens and soldiers from defeated nations were enslaved. The session Scripture text uses the practice of slavery to describe the role of the Christian before God, and the demeanor of Christians in a world hostile to them.

- Read 1 Peter 2:18–20. Note that verse 18 addresses those who are slaves. Jot down a list of the advice given to slaves. How does this advice apply to the early Christians? What are some pros and cons of comparing Christians to slaves?
- At times in history, Bible texts like this have been used to condone slavery. What do you think about this?

2. Scholars have conjectured that a portion of the session Scripture text has its origins in a hymn used by the early church. Others theorize that the language used does not support this, but instead reflects the writer's plentiful use of Old Testament references to make theological points.

- Review 1 Peter 2:22–25. Then, as Isaiah 53 is read aloud, raise your hand whenever you hear something similar to 1 Peter 2:22–25.

God's Own People Learner Guide

SESSION THREE

- What do you think—is 1 Peter 2:22-25 an early church hymn, a text that relies heavily on the Old Testament, or something else? Take a poll of people in your group.

Literary Context

1. Household codes were a popular form of literature in the first century. These codes described the duties and expected demeanor of every member of the Roman household (children, parents, spouses, and workers). The writer of 1 Peter uses this familiar literary genre to give churches advice for their situations.

- Read 1 Peter 2:18-22 and 3:1-7 and two other household codes in the Bible: Titus 2:1-10 and Ephesians 5:21-6:9. In as few words as possible, sum up the advice given to early Christians and their congregations.
- Write a "code" for your household. How does it compare to those you just read?

2. A major theme of the epistle emerges in 1 Peter 2:19-25. Earlier in the letter, the writer emphasizes the gifts that God has given the churches through Christ, and acknowledges their suffering. Then he states that the churches suffer like Christ suffered because this is their calling.

- Read the following texts and identify ways in which suffering may be part of following Jesus. How might we suffer for the gospel today?

    Matthew 8:18-22
    Matthew 16:24-26
    Mark 13:9-13
    Luke 12:51-53
    John 13:36-38

Lutheran Context

1. Lutherans believe that God speaks universal truths in scripture that are then applied to individual lives and communities. Because of this, we interpret scripture on a public level—with all people, over cultural and political boundaries, and even those separated from us by time.

- With this in mind, try paraphrasing 1 Peter 2:19-21. Use words and images that allow this text to speak to a modern audience, but also reflect the original "situation in life."

Notes

Session 3: 1 Peter 2:19–25   19

SESSION THREE

Notes

2. Lutherans test interpretations of scripture partly by working in community. The name of this series of studies—Together in Faith—reminds us that Bible study can't occur in a vacuum. It needs the breath of the Spirit as well as the voices of many. Only in partnership can we hope to discern the living truths waiting for us in, with, and under the printed words of the Bible.

- What types of different voices might provide insights into 1 Peter 2:19-25 that we cannot attain ourselves? Whose voices would you most like to hear? Why are their voices important to understanding this text?

Devotional Context

1. Jesus didn't suffer needlessly. He suffered because the kingdom he was ushering in upset worldly power structures and defied human avarice. His suffering and death were intended to destroy him, but instead established that kingdom's arrival.

- Read together "O Sacred Head, Now Wounded" (ELW 351 or 352). Spend several minutes in silence afterwards, thinking about the lyrics in relation to 1 Peter 2:19-25. Share insights.

2. Jesus' life and death on the cross model for us the Christian life, a life that includes suffering. Suffering for Jesus' sake can involve being rejected, ignored, misunderstood, defamed, slandered, and even physically harmed. There is also joy and fulfillment in Jesus' call, because of the resurrection. Ironically, suffering can bring us that joy when others are helped and experience Christ through it.

- Think about ways you and/or your congregation suffer for the gospel. What ministries do you support? How is God calling your congregation to suffer for others in your community?

Wrap-up

Be ready to look back over the work your group has done in this session.

Pray

Lord, in baptism we are marked with the cross of Christ, and you call us to a life that reflects that cross. As your son Jesus suffered for what was right, help us to boldly suffer for doing what is right in the name of Christ. Give us the courage and strength to take what we learned this day and put it into action. Amen.

Go in peace to serve the Lord. Remember you are baptized!

SESSION THREE

Extending the Conversation

Homework

1. Read the next session's Bible text: 1 Peter 2:2–10.

2. If you're on Facebook or Twitter, include one update each day that reflects your faith in Christ. This might be a comment advocating for those in need, or perhaps a prayer for a friend. Keep a journal of the responses you get and how they make you feel. (Another option is to do or say one thing a day to share your faith.)

3. Slavery still exists in the world with the recruiting, transporting, and harboring of people for forced labor or sexual exploitation. For more on the crime of human trafficking and what you can do to fight it, visit these Web sites:
The Not for Sale Campaign:
www.notforsalecampaign.org
U.S. Department of Health and Human Services:
www.acf.hhs.gov/trafficking
Canadian Department of Justice:
www.justice.gc.ca/eng/fs-sv/tp

4. Leaf through "Foxe's Book of Martyrs" by John Foxe (Revell, 1999) for stories of people who suffered as Christ did by dying for their faith. (Warning: some of these stories get quite grisly. Don't read them to children.)

Enrichment

1. Look up "call" in a Bible concordance and examine the call stories of some prophets, kings of Israel, disciples, and early Christians. How did these people suffer as they followed Christ? How might you?

2. Christians suffering from hostility towards them today include members of the Evangelical Lutheran Church in Jordan and the Holy Land. Find out more at www.elcjhl.org.

3. The writer of 1 Peter gives a poetic rendition of what is believed about Jesus. It's not exhaustive, but it relates directly to the situation at hand. Try writing a statement of beliefs or creed based on 1 Peter 2:19–25. Include any reminders about Jesus that your church or congregation might need at this time.

Notes

SESSION THREE

Notes

For Further Reading

A Better Freedom: Finding Life as Slaves of Christ by Michael Card (InterVarsity Press, 2009).

The Cost of Discipleship by Dietrich Bonhoeffer (Touchstone, 1995).

SESSION FOUR

1 Peter 2:2–10

Learner Session Guide

Focus Statement

God works in surprising ways! Like a rejected stone that becomes the cornerstone, Jesus' startling rejection is only surpassed by the equally astonishing power of his death and resurrection—the cornerstone of our salvation and proclamation as God's holy people.

Key Verse

But you are a chosen race, a royal priesthood, a holy nation, God's own people, in order that you may proclaim the mighty acts of him who called you out of darkness into his marvelous light.
1 Peter 2:9

A Holy People

 Focus Image

To make it more earthquake-resistant, no mortar was used in building this stone wall in Peru. © iStockphoto

Gather

Check-in

Welcome! Take this time to connect or reconnect with the others in your group. Be ready to share new thoughts or insights about your last session.

Pray

(This prayer is based on ELW 529, a hymn from Zimbabwe, "Jesus, We Are Gathered." Text/Tune Patrick Matsikenyiri © 1990, 1996 General Board of Global Ministries, GBG Musik.)

All: Jesus, we are gathered for you!
L: *Jesu, tawa pano.* (*Jesus, we are gathered. Pronunciation: jay-su, tau-wa pah-no.*)
P: *Jesu, tawa pano.*
L: *Jesu, tawa pano.*
P: *Jesu, tawa pano.*
L: *Jesu, tawa pano.*
P: *Jesu, tawa pano.*

Session 4: 1 Peter 2:2–10   23

SESSION FOUR

 Notes

L: *Tawa pano mu zita renyu. (We are gathered for you. Pronunciation: tau–wa pah–no meu zee–ta ray–nu.)*
P: *Tawa pano mu zita renyu.*
L: *Jesus, we are gathered here for you. Open our minds and tongues to discussion. Open our eyes and ears to your word, that we might be your holy people in the world. Amen.*

Focus Activity

Look at the Focus Image. The session Scripture text compares Jesus to a rock or stone. What do you think about this? Choose a word or title that describes Jesus in a meaningful way for you.

Open Scripture

Read 1 Peter 2:2–10.

- What images come to mind as you hear this text?

- What question would you ask the author of 1 Peter, if you could?

- What emotions do you experience as you hear this text? What words trigger these emotions?

Join the Conversation

Historical Context

1. Many early Christian communities were made up of former Jews and Gentiles (non–Jews), which led to some friction between Jewish synagogues and the people in these communities who remained Jewish in identity, but believed in Jesus as Messiah. The churches in Asia Minor, however, were more likely to have been made up of Gentiles, and thus faced a different challenge—tensions between Christianity and the Greco-Roman culture in that place and time. At the time 1 Peter was written, a good portion of the known world was under the domination of Rome. (See the map of the Roman Empire on the next page.)

SESSION FOUR

- Read 1 Peter 2:9-10. Discuss how these words might have sounded to Roman rulers, and to the people addressed by this letter.
- How does 1 Peter 2:9-10 sound to you? What, if any, effect does your situation or experience have on this?

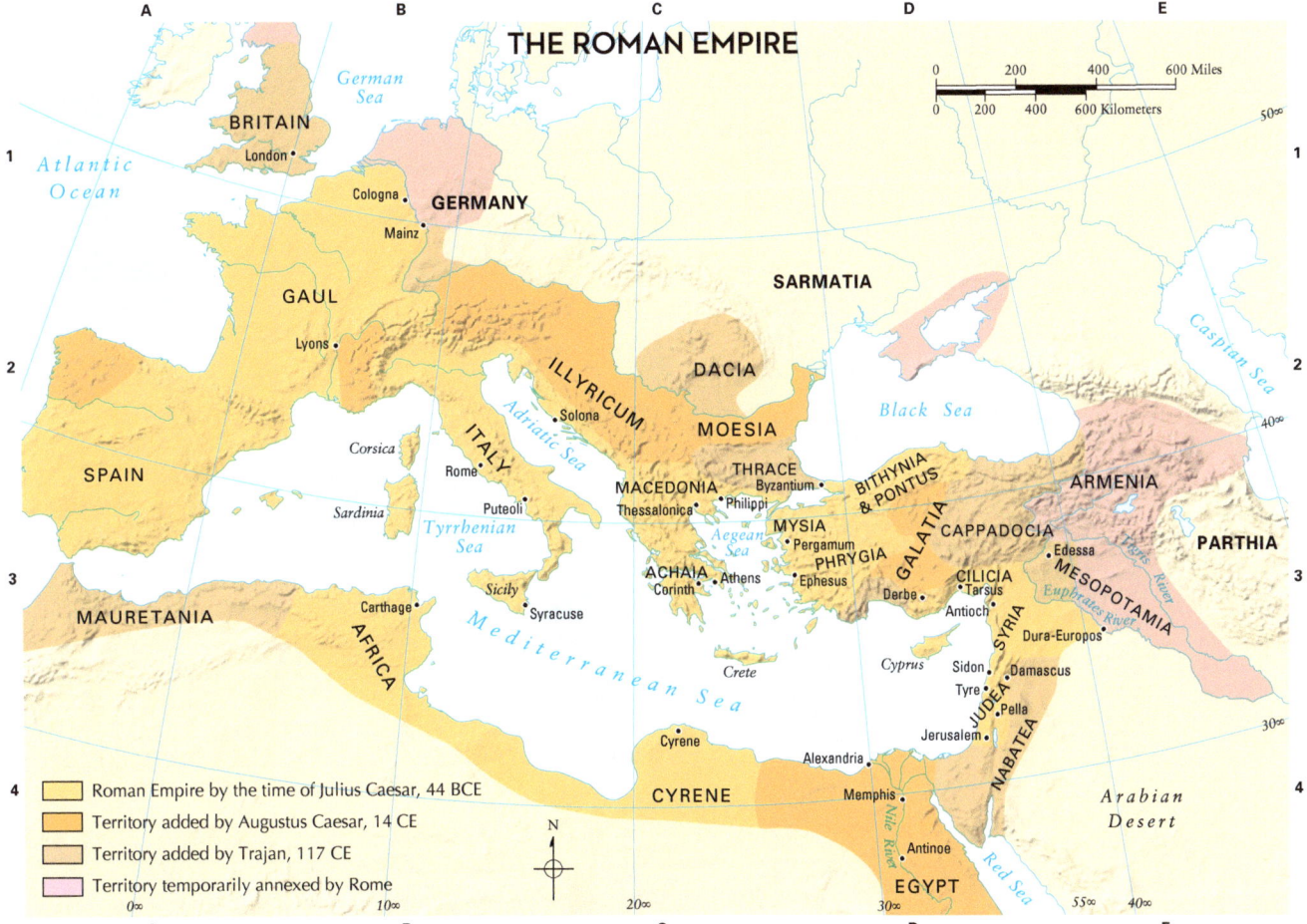

2. The Roman Empire was both skilled and prolific in its building of roads and other stone infrastructure, such as aqueducts and bridges. The people of Israel were also quite adept at stone work—the temple in Jerusalem stood in testimony to that. A cornerstone or foundation stone was the first stone put in place for a building's foundation. It became the reference point for laying stones for the rest of the building. The living stone in 1 Peter is Christ, but we are to be living stones as well, built into a spiritual house—the church. Jesus is the cornerstone of that house—a stone that can be built upon to form us into God's own people.

- List some reasons why the author of 1 Peter might have used the well-known imagery of the cornerstone to make his point about Jesus and the church.

SESSION FOUR

Notes

Literary Context

1. The session Scripture text draws heavily on Old Testament images and texts. Identify the words or phrases in 1 Peter 2:2–10 that relate to these Old Testament passages:

> Exodus 19:5–6
> Deuteronomy 32:18
> Psalm 33:9a
> Psalm 118:22
> Isaiah 8:14
> Isaiah 28:16
> Isaiah 43:20–21

2. The author of 1 Peter uses metaphors, figures of speech that draw on language from a different field or context. For example, in 1 Peter 2 the writer says the people are infants growing strong on mother's milk. This is not to say that the churches were like infants, or that the churches were spiritual infants. Rather, the writer compares the eagerness to grow as a Christian through the Word to the yearning of an infant for milk.

- Review 1 Peter 2:2–10 and identify any other metaphors that appear in this text.
- Brainstorm a list of other metaphors that could describe the joys and pitfalls of life as God's own people.

Lutheran Context

1. Priests in ancient Israel acted as mediators between God and the people, but Martin Luther taught that all people now have direct access to God through Jesus Christ, and are called to serve God and their neighbors. He based this teaching, called the priesthood of all believers, in part on 1 Peter 2. The author of 1 Peter, however, uses the concept of "a royal priesthood" to show similarities between Jesus and the early church. Jesus was the stone rejected by the builders that became the cornerstone. The people in Asia Minor are the church, the cornerstone of the proclamation of the gospel. They may experience rejection and persecution from the world, but they will always be God's own.

- Was Luther's understanding of the phrase "a royal priesthood" incorrect? What do you think?
- How can the words "a royal priesthood" mean one thing to the original listeners, and something else to someone who reads scripture hundreds of years later?

SESSION FOUR

2. One principle for Lutherans in reading and interpreting the Bible is "what shows forth Christ." Using this principle we ask, "What do we learn about the nature, role, and work of Christ from the text?"

- Look at 1 Peter 2:6–8. What does this passage say about Jesus through the metaphor of Christ as a stone, especially as a "living" stone?

Devotional Context

1. List hymns and songs that have "rock" or "stone" in the lyrics. How do these songs relate to the session Scripture text?
2. Write, doodle, or draw your response to this question: What do the images of Christ as a stone or rock and the church as "living stones" say to you, your congregation, and the world?

Wrap-up

Be ready to look back over the work your group has done in this session.

Pray

O Lord God, our rock, O Jesus, our living stone, make us your holy people, and in your mercy, hear our prayers. Amen.

Go in peace to serve the Lord. You are a holy people, called out of darkness into God's marvelous light!

Extending the Conversation

Homework

1. Read the next session's Bible text: 1 Peter 3:13–22.

2. The imagery of Christians yearning for the word of God as an infant yearns for milk is a powerful metaphor that reminds us of our need for spiritual growth—at all ages. Form or support a "cradle roll" program in your congregation to keep track of newborns and support the spiritual growth of parents and children by contacting them at major milestones in the baby's life (first steps, birthdays, etc.).

3. Do an impromptu survey after worship, asking people, "As God's own holy people, what is the most exciting way we proclaim God's word at (name of your congregation)?" Share the responses with the pastor and committees in the congregation.

 Notes

SESSION FOUR

4. Help your group or a Sunday school class memorize scripture by making 1 Peter 2:10 into a call and response (or song). (For example, the leader might say, "Once you were not a people," and everyone might respond, "but now we are God's people!") If you wish, come up with other "Once you…but now…" verses based on Scripture.

Enrichment

1. The children's book *Stone Soup* by Marcia Brown (Atheneum, 2010) tells the story of some poor soldiers who build a soup on a stone, and build up sharing in a small town as well. Read this story and think about how the soup stone and the living stone are similar. Plan a Stone Soup supper and invite guests to bring something for the soup pot. Read the story aloud as you wait for the cooperative meal to cook. Consider making a donation to fight world hunger in response to this experience of sharing!

2. Do some research on stone cutting and construction, or visit a stone quarry if possible.

For Further Reading

The Cup of Our Life: A Guide to Spiritual Growth by Joyce Rupp (Ave Maria Press, 1997).

Open the Doors and See All the People: Stories of Church Identity and Vocation by Norma Cook Everist (Augsburg Fortress, 2004).

SESSION FIVE

1 Peter 3:13–22

Learner Session Guide

Focus Statement

Baptized into the death and resurrection of Jesus Christ, tested and made new and holy, and trusting in God's mercy, we stand ready to proclaim the power of God in our lives.

Key Verse

Always be ready to make your defense to anyone who demands from you an accounting for the hope that is in you. 1 Peter 3:15b

A Proclaiming People

 Focus Image

We are baptized into the death and resurrection of Jesus Christ. © Design Pics/SuperStock

Gather

Check-in

Welcome! Take this time to connect or reconnect with the others in your group. Be ready to share new thoughts or insights about your last session.

Pray

Make us eager, O God, to tell the story of your love and grace. Make us ready to share our faith with others, and prepare us to speak to injustice in this world. Make us impatient for the coming kingdom. Be with us and let our discussions run deep and our respect for each other run wide. Be with us and help us understand your love for us more fully, and desire more of the knowledge and comfort that comes from reading your word. Amen.

Focus Activity

Take a minute to complete the following sentence. Write down as many things as you can, whether they sound "religious" or not.

    I believe ….

Now look at the Focus Image. What do the people in the photo believe?

Session 5: 1 Peter 3:13–22   29

SESSION FIVE

Notes

Open Scripture
Read 1 Peter 3:13–22.

- How does this passage make you feel?

- What words or images stand out to you?

- What does this passage motivate you to do?

Join the Conversation
Historical Context

1. "Jesus Christ" was the first Christian creed or statement of belief about Jesus and his identity. It assigned the Hebrew title of *Messiah* or the anointed one (*Christos* in Greek) to Jesus of Nazareth. Other creedal statements followed. Bits and pieces of early church "Christ hymns" and Old Testament prophecies evolved into statements of belief, and epistle writers like Paul and the author of 1 Peter drew from this material.

- Look at 1 Peter 3:18–22. Underline the phrases that may have been part of early Christian creeds. What is said about Jesus? Compare this with the Apostles' Creed, which is often used in worship today.

2. There is ample evidence that the author of 1 Peter believed that Jesus would return soon to judge the people and trigger the creation of a new world order. He wanted the people to be ready for that day, and gave them advice on living in the meantime.

- We also live in the time in between Jesus' first coming and second coming, yet we don't necessarily feel the same urgency. How might people in the early church and today follow the advice of 1 Peter?

SESSION FIVE

	Then	Now
Do what is right.		
Do not be intimidated.		
Be ready to make your defense.		
Suffer for doing good, if necessary.		
Witness with gentleness and reverence.		

 Notes

Literary Context

1. The author hinges the body of his epistle on the meaning and purpose of the suffering the people are experiencing at the hands of their pagan society and culture. With Christ as their model, the people may suffer for doing good, and they should be ready to "defend" themselves by proclaiming their "hope."

- If you created a series of bumper stickers for cars based on 1 Peter 3:13–22, what would you say? Boil down the text and its themes to their essence by writing three "bumper sticker" slogans. (Use as few words as possible.)

2. The session Scripture text, 1 Peter 3:13–22, has a larger literary context. As part of the main body of 1 Peter, this text contains part of the main argument of the epistle. In the New Testament, the text fits in with the gospels and with other letters in proclaiming Jesus Christ as Lord. In the Bible as a whole, the text fits with overall biblical themes such as the suffering of the righteous, being blessed by God, and being saved through water and God's word.

- When you read Bible passages, do you usually think about them on their own, as part of a larger book, or part of the entire Bible? Discuss what difference it makes to think about a text as part of something bigger.

Lutheran Context

1. Lutherans read the Bible through the lenses of law and gospel. Because we are unable to live up to it, the law drives us to Christ. In the gospel, we hear what 1 Peter calls the "hope that is in you"—the good news of God in Christ Jesus.

SESSION FIVE

Notes

- Identify law and gospel in 1 Peter 3:13-22, then discuss how we are to respond to the law and the gospel.

2. Read Martin Luther's explanation of baptism (*Small Catechism*, pp. 28-30, or ELW, pp. 1164-1165) and identify what baptism does. What aspects of baptism are emphasized in the session Scripture text by referring to Noah and his family?

Devotional Context

1. The author of 1 Peter gives the churches some thoughtful pastoral care and advice. He is concerned not only for their physical well-being, but also their spiritual health—the condition of their faith. The result is almost prayer-like.

- Read the text for today once more and write down words or phrases that demonstrate this care for the churches' well-being. Write a prayer for those who suffer, using this language and imagery.

2. Choose a word or phrase based on the session Scripture text, such as "Jesus suffered," "once for all," or "the righteous for the unrighteous." Meditate on this word or phrase for a few moments—close your eyes if you wish and repeat the words slowly to yourself. Write, draw, or doodle any words or images that come to mind.

Wrap-up

Be ready to look back over the work your group has done in this session.

Pray

Loving God, we come to you broken and sinful, with nothing to offer in return for your love. We give thanks that you have made us whole and blameless in your sight, through Jesus Christ, your Son and our Lord. Amen.

May God bless and keep you as you continue to explore Scripture!

Extending the Conversation
Homework

1. Read 1 Peter in its entirety. Outline the letter as you read it. (One way to do this is to imagine you are making 1 Peter into a movie. What would make up Part One, Part Two, Scene Three, the Epilogue, etc.?) Keep the outline in your Bible for future reference.

SESSION FIVE

2. The study goes on! Visit your church or local library and find a one-volume commentary on the Bible (HarperCollins publishes one, for example) and a commentary dedicated to 1 Peter. Skim through these. Slow down to read more carefully the sections that most interest you.

Enrichment

1. Write an account of your faith life. Include spiritual events, such as baptism, and life events that resulted in you questioning your faith or growing in faith. Be succinct, but be sure to convey the impact that faith in Jesus has had in your life. Review what you have written many times, making note of the transitions and stories. Then practice telling your story without any notes.

2. The movie *Romero* (Paulist Pictures, 1989) tells the story of Archbishop Oscar Romero, who was not afraid to suffer and even die for his belief in Christ and for his opposition to the oppressive government of El Salvador. Watch the movie with some friends who don't attend Bible study. Discuss the parts of the movie that move you. Invite your friends to join you in growing in knowledge of Scripture.

3. Read quickly through 2 Peter, comparing it to 1 Peter as you go. Do some research on the story behind this epistle.

For Further Reading

The Apostles' Creed: A User's Guide by Marshall D. Johnson (Augsburg Books, 2008).

Baptism: A User's Guide by Martin E. Marty (Augsburg Books, 2008).

Early Christian Creeds by J.N.D. Kelly, third ed. (Continuum, 2006).

Evangelism for 'Normal' People: Good News for Those Looking for a Fresh Approach by John P. Bowen (Augsburg Fortress, 2002).

 Notes

Printed in the USA
CPSIA information can be obtained
at www.ICGtesting.com
LVHW071953041024
792058LV00030B/22